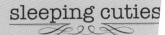

sleeping cuties

CW00369924

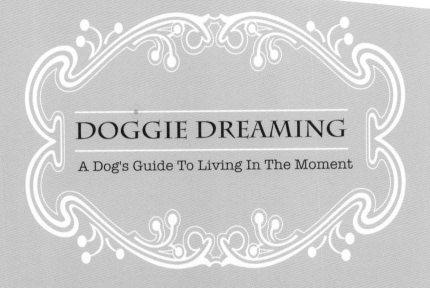

DOGGIE DREAMING

A Dog's Guide To Living In The Moment

David & Heidi Cuschieri

First Edition 2013

National Library of Australia
Cataloguing-in-Publication entry:

Doggie Dreaming: A Dog's Guide To Living In The Moment / David and Heidi Cuschieri

1st ed.
ISBN 9780987299321 (pbk.)

Sleeping Cuties series

Dogs.
Dogs--Effect of human beings on.
Dogs--Social aspects.
Dogs--Behaviour.

636.7

Published by The Next Big Think
Printed and bound in Hong Kong
For further information about orders:
Email: info@the-next-big-think.com
Website: www.the-next-big-think.com

DOGS KNOW THE
SECRET TO HAPPINESS
IS TO LIVE IN THE
PRESENT MOMENT.

Live The Life Of Your Dreams Now

If you spend time with dogs you may very well discover a little secret that they have known since time immemorial. They know the secret to happiness and practise what they have discovered daily.

Dogs have been our constant companions for as long as we can remember. We need only look into our puppy dog's eyes to glimpse true happiness. Dogs know instinctively that happiness exists right now. While we are busy planning and wishing for future happiness, and for our dreams to come true, dogs are working on being happy right now simply by living in the present moment.

It is important to dream and work towards them, but it is also equally important to be conscious of every moment of your life right now. It is easy to get lost in thought and miss out on the incredible beauty that is right in front of your nose now. In fact, stop what you are doing right now, take a deep breath, exhale slowly and begin to get in tune with your body. Feel your clothing touching your skin. Feel your heart beating. Listen to the sounds around you right now. Rather than get lost in thought, immerse yourself in your senses.

Waking up and smelling the roses is about getting out of your mind and back into your body. Dogs have a keen sense of smell and maybe we too can learn to take great pleasure in being lost in our senses. So much so that when someone asks you how you are you could answer 'sensational!'.

The nomadic Australian Aborigines' constant and loyal companion was the dingo. Aborigines were hunter-gatherers, and moved from place to place, becoming acutely aware and in tune with their surroundings. They moved with the seasons and the availability of food and water, and had stories of how their land was created known as The Dreamtime. It wasn't some time in the distant past but the here and now. The Dreamtime is about the continual process of creation and we too have the power to dream and create this very moment.

I think there was a time when we all used to know the secret of happiness. It was a time when humans sat around the campfire with their canine companions and listened and learned from their companion's wisdom.

Doggie Dreaming is a guide to help you understand that The Dreamtime is here and now and happiness is available to you in this very moment. Think less, appreciate the little things in your life now, and spend time around dogs. Have you ever seen a dog when his master has come home? He isn't worried about what is happening on the stock market or listening to gossip as he wags his tail. While you were lost in thought he was blissfully lost in living his dreams. The secret to the art of living and happiness is to see the magic in every moment for now has always been when and where we create the life of our dreams.

When we pause awhile
we realise that life isn't all
black and white but filled
with many shades of grey.
At these moments we
become filled with
'greytitude'.

A concrete
jungle
can be a field of
flowers
when we have
appreciation
in our
hearts.

Inspiration is closing your eyes
and taking it all in.

Every
dream
began with a
big idea
followed by many
tiny steps
in between many
sleeps.

The secret to
happiness
is to be in
'the zone'
as much as possible,
even if sometimes it
gets you in a mess.

It is the
simple things
that can give us the
greatest joy,
like the company
of others.

Dreams

are not what you
leave behind when
morning comes,
they are the stuff that
fill your every living

moment.

Thinking
less

doesn't make you
thoughtless.

Life isn't so
'Aggghhhhhfull!'
after a big almighty yawn.

You know that
you are truly
alive
when you spend
less time
doing
and more time
being.

It is important to
slow down
but not so much
that you can't
get up again.

Illness
can be a
gift
and a reality check,
helping us realise
what really is
important in
life.

There's no **time** like the present.

Choose today to
to focus on bringing
joy to others.

Do something small
to make someone else

smile

so they know that there
is someone who has
thought about them.

The little things are
the big things that
make every day
extra special.

We can open the
door
to our greatest
dreams,
when we let go
and let things
happen.

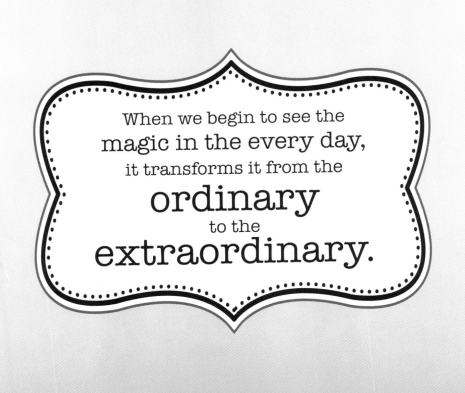

When we begin to see the
magic in the every day,
it transforms it from the
ordinary
to the
extraordinary.

Put
less on
your plate
is a good
lesson.

Regardless of
what happens today
I'm going to have an
awesome day.
No, not 'some awe'
but 'full of awe'.
In fact, I'm going
to have a totally
'awe-full' day!

Every morning
I make the biggest
decision of my life:
to be happy today.
All I know is the
here and now.
What happened
yesterday is gone,
what may happen
tomorrow hasn't
happened yet.

The mind is a powerful force.
It can enslave us or empower us.
It can plunge us into the depths of misery or take us to the heights of ecstasy.
Learn to use the power wisely.

The easiest way to be

happy

is to let go of having to
control everything in
your life in every
moment.

Today I choose
to be out of my
mind
and more in my
heart
- isn't this what being
insanely happy
is all about?

When we let go of blame and take responsibility, we give ourselves the ability to respond to life's challenges in ways that help us grow and can show us the path to happiness.

At the end of each day ask yourself:

Did I make someone smile?
Did I learn something new?
Was I grateful for today?

If you said yes to any of these questions you know that today you have lived.

Let go of thinking about what you **don't** have and instead shine a light on all that you **do**.
It is then that you will allow space for good things to enter.

Fear.

Sometimes the only thing
that is stopping us from
living the life of our dreams
is the stuff between our ears.

Today

your life is
ripe for the
living.

Sometimes the **happiest moments** of our lives are the ones when we appreciate what is right in front of us right now.

You cannot really
ever possess anything
more precious than
this very moment.

When we close our eyes
we can see our dreams.
The secret to living is to
see and live them with
our eyes open.

An impatient person

counts

the seconds.

A happy person

enjoys

the moment.

If a fly is called a 'fly'
because it can fly,
then why aren't
'human beings' called
'human doings'?

Close your eyes
and remember
that life is a

dream

- the secret is
to live it as
consciously
as possible.

Your body contains
infinite
wisdom.

Listen more to your body
and less to your mind.

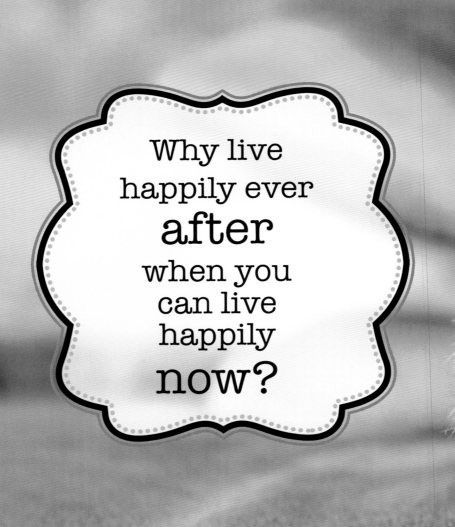

Why live
happily ever
after
when you
can live
happily
now?

There is always time for a

cuppa.

Thank You

We have brought together our words and the images of others, to send out special messages to touch the hearts and lives of people the world over.

Thank you to all who have made this book possible - the people who have touched our lives so that we could write the words of wisdom that fill these pages; the photographers who's images give us joy and wonder; the printers for their attention to detail and assistance; the distributors for their guidance, passion and belief; the retailers for their support; and last but not least, to the gift givers and receivers who will pay it forward and carry on the essence of what our gift books are all about.

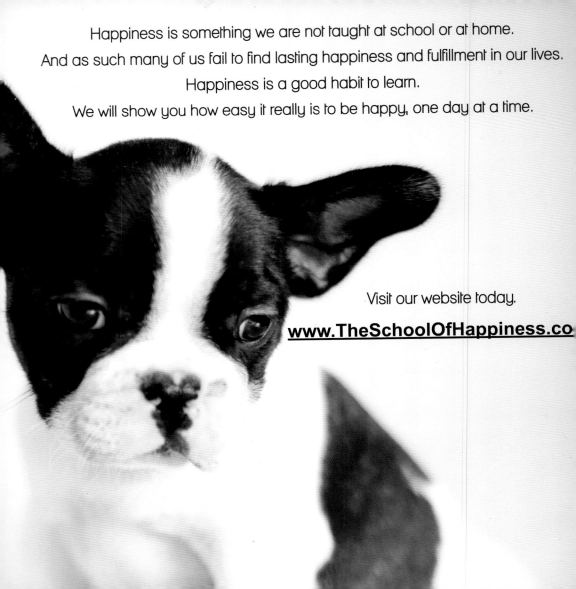

Happiness is something we are not taught at school or at home.
And as such many of us fail to find lasting happiness and fulfillment in our lives.
Happiness is a good habit to learn.
We will show you how easy it really is to be happy, one day at a time.

Visit our website today.
www.TheSchoolOfHappiness.co